THERE IS NO ASS EATING IN HERE.

What is Wrong With You Pervert

Made in the USA
Las Vegas, NV
30 November 2023

81813637R00069